Lifetimes

A beautiful way to explain death to children

LIFETIMES
A Bantam Book/October 1983

ISBN 0-553-34023-9

Published simultaneously in the United States and Canada

PRINTED AND BOUND IN SINGAPORE
THROUGH HEDGES AND BELL (S.E. ASIA)

0   9   8   7   6   5   4   3   2   1

Lifetimes

A beautiful way to explain death to children

Bryan Mellonie and Robert Ingpen

BANTAM BOOKS
TORONTO · NEW YORK · LONDON · SYDNEY

There is a beginning
and an ending for everything
that is alive.
In between is living.

Nest with new laid eggs

All around us, everywhere,
beginnings and endings
are going on all the time.

Broken periwinkle shells

With living in between.

Lion fish of the coral reef

This is true for all living things.

For plants.

For people.

For birds.

For fish.

For trees.

For animals.

Even for

the tiniest insect.

Nothing that is alive
goes on living for ever.
How long it lives depends upon
what it is and what happens
while it is living.

Dead sand crab

Sometimes, living things become ill
or they get hurt.
Mostly, of course, they get better again
but there are times when they are so badly hurt
or they are so ill that they die because
they can no longer stay alive.

This can happen when they are young,
or old, or anywhere in between.

Remains of a butterfly

It may be sad, but it is the way
of all things, and it is true
for everything that is alive.
For plants.
For people.
For birds.
For fish.
For trees.
For animals.

Even for
the tiniest insect.

There are lots of living things
in our world.
Each one has its own special lifetime.

Young apple growing

Trees that are tall and strong
grow slowly, standing in the sunshine
and in the rain.
Some of them live for a very long
time indeed, as long as a hundred
years or more.
That is their lifetime.

Old grape vine budding

Rabbits and mice grow up in only
a few weeks. Then they go on to live
for a year or two, crunching up carrots
and nibbling at cheese until they grow
old and very tired and it is
their time to die.
That is how it happens to be
for rabbits and mice.
It is the way they live, and it is their lifetime.

Rabbit and mouse living

Flowers and vegetables, planted as
seeds at the beginning of Spring when
the earth is warm, grow quickly
to live through the heat of Summer.
The days pass and they become old
during Autumn when it is cooler.
Then, when Winter comes and it is cold,
they die.
It is the way they live.
That is their lifetime.

Butterflies live as butterflies
for only a few weeks. Once they have
dried their wings, they flutter and flit
from leaf to flower. At first, they are
bright and quick, but as time passes
they begin to slow down until finally
they can go no further. They rest for
a while, and then they die.
That is the way butterflies live, and
that is their lifetime.

Butterfly resting

Birds grow up quite quickly, too.
It is often no more than a few months
from the time they hatch until they are
strong enough to fly and feed themselves.
How long they live after that seems to depend
upon their size. Mostly, the bigger they are,
the longer they will be alive.
That is the way birds live:
some for as long as fifty years,
others no more than two or three.
But, however long, it is their lifetime
for each one.

Kookaburra and Emu wren of Australia

Fish, swimming in lakes and rivers
or in the sea, can be so tiny it is hard to tell
that they are there at all, or so big that the
only way to describe them is enormous.
Again, as far as we know, it seems that
the smaller they are, the shorter will be
their lifetime, but that is how it is for fish.
Their lives can be as little as a day or so,
or as long as eighty or ninety years.
It is the way they live,
and those are their lifetimes.

School of startled anchovy

And people?

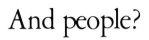

Well, like everything else that is alive,
people have lifetimes, too.
They live for about sixty or seventy years,
sometimes even longer, doing all the things
that people do like growing up
and being grown up.

Four generations

It can happen, though, just as it does with
all other living things, that people
become ill or they get hurt.
Mostly, of course, they get better again
but there are times when they are so badly
hurt or they are so ill that they die
because they can no longer stay alive.
It may be sad, but that is how it is
for people. It is the way they live
and it is their lifetime.

Just a splinter!

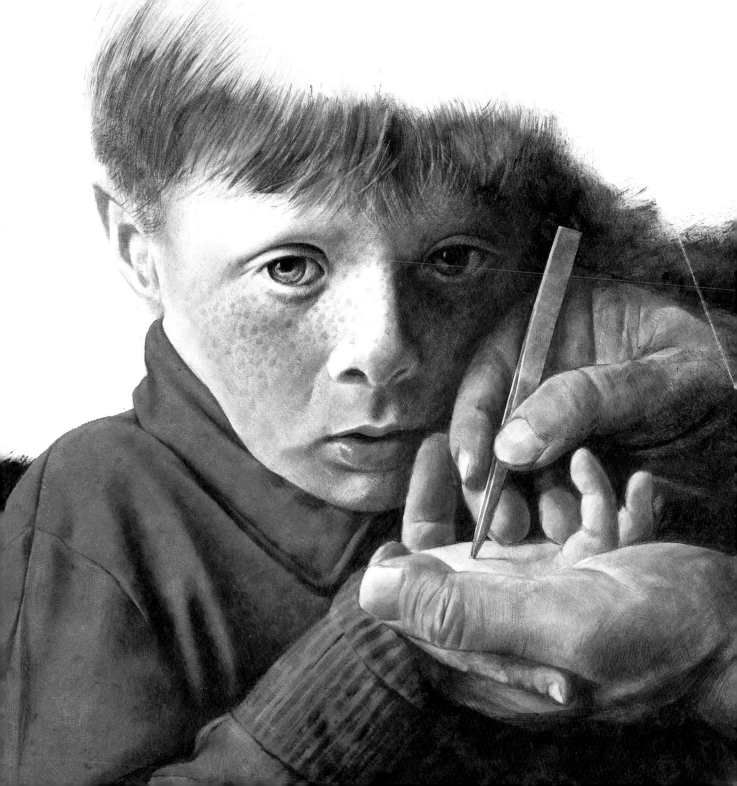

So, no matter how long they are,
or how short, lifetimes are really
all the same.
They have beginnings, and endings,
and there is living in between.

That is how things are.

For plants.

For people.

For birds.

For fish.

For animals.

Even for the tiniest insects.

EVERYWHERE!